C000146412

poems

AFTER THE ASHES

e.v. nova

harbor lane books

AFTER THE ASHES
Copyright © 2023 by E.V. Nova

Published in the United States of America by Harbor Lane Books, LLC.

www.harborlanebooks.com

Dedication

to anyone who's ever been broken by love,
you're strong,
you're worthy,
and you're enough.
it took 184 days for me to catch my first glimpse of the sun,
and you will, too.
we live, we learn...and still, we love.

your freedom put me in a cage,
and still, i would throw away the key for you.

a house of lies mistaken for truth.
a mouth full of silence disguised as honesty.
a stranger's eyes veiled by familiarity.
a heart disfigured by a life that maybe never was.
this is home.

the clouds roll in,
as does my grief,
surprising me with a renewed lightning strike of despair
and the thunderous roar of my tears.

the painful hole in my heart inflicted by you eerily resembles the shape of your love.

your love cuts like a rusty knife,
leaving jagged, disfiguring scars.
i reach out for you,
but all you can see is the mess my blood is making on your floor.

you use your love of shiny metal and excessive speed
to mask the dullness in your eyes and sluggish beating of your
dying heart,
the same way i use my love of pretty written words to hide the
broken promises assaulting my ears and the memories trapped
within the pages of my own tragic story.

the version of me before you is gone,
yet the version of me without you yearns to remember her,
and mourns her loss,
just as she mourns the loss of you—the you, you used to be.
or rather, the you, you made her believe you were.

you say you've fallen out of love with me.
how, when you don't know the me i've become
while i've waited for you?
while i picked up your laundry and you swallowed your words.
while i scalded my hands in dishwater and you kept yours tucked
safely away,
along with your heart.
while my eyes seared from tears and your gaze looked past me
without wanting to see.
how can you fall out of love with someone you've both forgotten
and never knew?

sometimes your words give me hope.

too much, bringing buoyancy and light.

other times you speak and it drags me below the surface of my own despair.

i could say those words mean everything.

i could say those words mean nothing.

but what i remember most vividly is that you used those same lips

to lie to me.

and those are the words that won't let me go.

sit down.
listen.
you'll hear it,
the screaming of my heart.
but it's not in my chest.
it's in the palm of your hand
and you're crushing it,
breaking it into unrecognizable pieces.
killing it.
killing us.

the cold creeps in
despite the warmth of your body against mine
because your touch is strange, unfamiliar,
bearing no resemblance to the man i used to know,
the man i used to love,
and who used to love me.

you smoke me out into the open with your pretty words and
promises,
then snuff me out with your lies.

you said you loved me,
then you said you didn't.
both times i believed you,
so much it hurt.

in marriage, you play for keeps.
just like marbles.
only you don't see me as something shiny,
something in the palm of your hand that you hold tightly,
afraid to let it go.
but you do hold me in your hand,
letting me slip through your fingers,
seeing me as a conglomerate of your mistakes and shortcomings,
disguised as my own.

my thoughts are punctured
by the broken pieces of my heart.
my heart is charred
by ignited gasoline poured on my soul.
my soul is diminished to dust,
murdered by the love you stole
and skillfully laid to rest
in a hole dug in the backyard of your past,
left to decay,
to become nothing,
just as I am to you.

if i had thought for one minute
that you would leave me the way you did,
i would have smashed the glass
and ripped the hands from the clock,
stopped the incessant ticking of time,
stopped you,
saved me.

the words i long to hear from you
are trapped somewhere deep inside you,
eclipsed by the shininess of her,
obstructed by the decades of us,
taken away by your desire for what i'll never be.

the words you text her,
they scar me.
the thoughts you think of her,
they sear my mind.
you haven't touched her
but you've dreamed of it
while lying beside me, so far away.
your dreams have become my nightmares.

your thoughts of her permeate mine.
they poison me.
yet i yearn for them to infiltrate me deeper,
to penetrate my very being the way she did you,
to make me more like her,
because then you'd think of me, too.

a key turns in the lock,
no forced entry.
but you're not welcome
because it's not entry you forced upon me.
it's heartbreak.
neglect.
regret.
i should have never let you in.

she touches you
when i'm in the room with you.
she whispers your name, clear and intoxicating,
when i beg for you to hear me at all.
the scent of her lingers in the air
though she has never been within these four walls.
she's everywhere, and nowhere,
a vampire feeding on the essence of us
because you invited her in.

we cannot sift through the ashes of our love when you're fueling the fire with her.

that flame will always look brighter when compared to the charred remains of us,

which you burnt to the ground.

she's not here, but she's everywhere.
just as you're standing before me,
but you're gone.

i never knew it was possible
to love someone too much.
but maybe loving at all is too much,
because when you realize
they maybe never loved you at all,
it's not the truth that shatters you.
it's your own love, broken,
being choked to death by its own trembling hand.

it's so confusing to feel so alone
and yet so relentlessly haunted
by your memory that won't let me go.

like the breadcrumbs strewn across the counter
and the laundry piled on the floor,
the bruises on my mind and the scars unseen
are reminders that you did only what you wanted,
a necessity to sustain yourself,
with no regard for the mess you left me in your wake.

this freedom tastes bitter,
but now i know why.
you fed me poison on a silver spoon to get it.

maybe i was wrong.
maybe i was never yours,
just as you were never mine,
and love was never ours.
maybe, just maybe,
we were never us
at all.

you'll have to excuse my inability to trust
the well wishes that roll off the same tongue
you used to utter those seductive words to her,
to call me crazy for asking if there was someone else,
to manipulate my mind and bend me to your will,
all while claiming to still love me.

i am your afterthought,
your used to be.
i'm your once was everything,
now i'm nothing.
i'm what you said you wanted,
what you said you were sure of.
the only thing i'm sure of is that someday you'll realize what i
really am...
your could have been.
your should have been.
but by then, i'll be your never will be.

there are two secrets you and i share.
one is the sheer enormity of your cruelty,
the other is just how unconditional my love truly was.

the bright flame flickers,
then transforms to pink,
while i pour out my soul
with scratches of ink.
i tell all my secrets
and speak of your lies,
but it's my own scarred heart
that in the moonlight still cries.

don't judge me
by my mistakes.
after all,
you were one of them.

you could have said you loved me.
you could have said you're sorry.
you could have said anything,
the bitter truth or a mouthful of lies,
but you chose to say nothing at all.
stark silence.
and in the deafening void of sound,
you said everything i needed to know.

i want to catch your words in my outstretched palms
as they fall like raindrops from your tongue,
not only so they don't stab me like needles in the heart,
but to revisit them when i need them,
to remind me why i don't need you.

there's a shocking sense of inclusion and freedom i've found
in being alone,
away from the stifling crowds of people who suffocated my soul
and made me feel lonely in their presence.

i asked myself in a whisper,
"why do you give him
your time,
your effort,
your patience,
your trust,
yet you will not offer yourself the same?"
my only answer was a single tear
and a devastating scream.

i would rather slice my skin
and watch the river run red
than see myself through your lying eyes
ever again.

always an audience watching me fail,
scratching scars into my psyche with a rusty nail.
now the veil has been lowered,
the hot tears let loose.
in the silence and solitude,
i can't hide from the truth.
with only my broken pieces for company,
i'll swallow the fire and let it burn.
when the flames die inside me and only ashes remain,
i'll rise and whisper through the smoke,
"now, it's my turn."

my last day in our broken home,
i took a meal from the freezer that your mother made.
i'd always loved your mom's home cooking.
today, i pulled it from my own freezer,
heated it, let it nourish me.
it tasted different somehow, bland.
it wasn't as good as i thought it would be.
in that way, it was a lot like you.
maybe my tastes have changed,
or maybe i've changed.
because now, neither that meal or you are to my tastes at all.

i am not a remnant of us,
something you discarded, left behind.
i am not a piece of glass never to be glued back together with
gold.
i am the gold.
i am the glitter of that glass as it catches the sun.
and you, you are the skin that i've shed,
far too small and dull to contain the beauty of my body
and the passion of my heart.

if i had to lose you
to find me,
then i'm sorry, sweetheart,
but i'm considering that a win.
then again, i'm not really sorry,
and i didn't really lose.

the light of hope can be found in the darkness of loss.
we must only feel our way through it to find it.

i use my pen to describe my scars.
not to highlight them for the world to see,
but to remind myself that i survived the wounds
and lived to tell about it.

do not ever mistake the love that courses through my veins like
lightning
for weakness.
it is that love which gave me the will
to survive the storm of you.

you are not your self-destructive thoughts.
but you are the one who's able to destroy them.

i waited for you,
and left myself hastily behind.
i believed in you,
and whispered lies to myself.
i craved your touch,
and pushed myself away.
i was so desperate to find a way to you
that i lost myself.
never again.

the sweetest revenge
is a woman scorned
remembering what it means
to be a woman adored.

my memories are of him.
my fantasies are of you.
but my now is me, only me,
because he left me behind,
and you just haven't found me yet.

it's hard to believe
there was a time when i believed your lies,
when i believed it was the end,
a time when i believed in nothing.
especially now,
when i've found a reason to believe in love again.

About the Author

E.V. Nova is a Canadian author and poet with a love for raw, devastatingly beautiful words. She believes in the power of turning pain into poetry, just as much as she believes everything happens for a reason. *After The Ashes* is her first published poetry collection.

Connect with E.V. Nova on Instagram and Facebook @evnovaofficial.

About the Publisher

Harbor Lane Books, LLC is a US-based independent, digital publisher of commercial fiction, non-fiction, and poetry.

Connect with Harbor Lane Books on their website www.harborlanebooks.com and TikTok, Instagram, Facebook, Twitter, and Pinterest @harborlanebooks.

Ingram Content Group UK Ltd.
Milton Keynes UK
UKHW010421150623
423468UK00003B/16